X-Treme Sports

In-Line Skating

Kristin Van Cleaf

ABDO Publishing Company

visit us at
www.abdopub.com

Published by ABDO Publishing Company, 4940 Viking Drive, Edina, Minnesota 55435.
Copyright © 2003 by Abdo Consulting Group, Inc. International copyrights reserved in all
countries. No part of this book may be reproduced in any form without written permission from
the publisher.

Printed in the United States.

Cover Photo: Corbis
Interior Photos: AP/Wide World p. 8; Corbis pp. 5, 6, 7, 9, 11, 13, 14, 15, 16, 17, 19, 21, 24-25,
    26, 27, 29, 31; Painet p. 12

Editors: Kate A. Conley, Stephanie Hedlund, Jennifer R. Krueger
Art Direction: Neil Klinepier

Library of Congress Cataloging-in-Publication Data

Van Cleaf, Kristin, 1976-
    In-line skating / Kristin Van Cleaf.
        p. cm. -- (X-treme sports)
    Includes index.
    Summary: Examines the history, techniques, racing events, and more of in-line skating.
    ISBN 1-57765-927-9
    1. In-line skating--Juvenile literature. [1. In-line skating.] I. Title. II. Series.

GV859.73 V36 2003
796.21--dc21
                                                                2002028330

Contents

In-Line Skating 4

The Beginning 6

The Skate 10

Gearing Up 14

Rules of the Road 18

Maintenance 20

Lingo 22

Fabiola da Silva 26

In-Line Skating Today 28

Glossary 30

Web Sites 31

Index 32

In-Line Skating

The first in-line skates were invented in France in the 1800s. Since the creation of those first skates, in-line skating has undergone many changes. Today, millions of people are stair riding, swizzling, and grinding in this exciting sport!

In-line skating is easy to learn. A beginner can take a course to learn the basics. At first, a new skater may feel nervous. But with practice, he or she will discover a great way to exercise and have fun!

The best in-line skaters practice often. Many skaters have worked to develop their sport. They participate in the Gravity Games, the X Games, and other competitions.

In-line skating has developed into other sports, too. These sports include in-line hockey, in-line speed skating, and aggressive skating. But millions of people also in-line skate just for fun.

The Beginning

Roller-skating and in-line skating have a shared history. For years, people have tried different ways of putting wheels on their feet. One of the world's first roller skates was invented in the 1700s. A Belgian inventor named Joseph Merlin designed this early skate.

In 1760, Merlin entered a party in London, England, wearing his skates and playing a violin. Unfortunately, Merlin hadn't thought of a way to stop! He crashed into a mirror, breaking both the mirror and his violin.

A Frenchman named Petitbled patented the first in-line skate in 1819. Petitbled's skate featured a wooden sole with leather straps. It had three wheels that could be made of ivory, metal, or wood. People could move forward with these skates, but turning was difficult.

A sketch of an 1861 in-line skate

As time went on, other people continued to improve the skate's design. Roller-skating eventually gained popularity with the development of the quad skate. In this design, each skate had four wheels. Two wheels were placed side-by-side in the front of the skate. The other two wheels were placed side-by-side in the back of the skate. This made moving and turning much easier.

In the 1960s, the Chicago Roller Skate Company created an in-line skate similar to those used today. However, these skates were not very comfortable. They were also unstable and had poor brakes.

In the 1970s, roller skaters began aggressive skating with small ramps and jumps. The sport has changed a lot since then.

7

Bob Naegele Jr.

Scott and Brennan Olson of Minnesota are credited with creating today's in-line skate. They wanted a way to train for ice hockey during the summer months. So in the early 1980s, they developed an in-line skate similar to a hockey skate.

Scott Olson eventually bought the patent for the Chicago Roller Skate Company's design. He continued to improve it. His changes included a plastic boot, better wheels and **bearings**, and a heel brake. Olson called his skate the Rollerblade.

Olson began **marketing** Rollerblades across the country. His skates quickly became a popular new item. In 1984, businessman Bob Naegele Jr. bought Olson's company. Rollerblade, Inc. continued to improve the skate's design. Eventually, other companies started making in-line skates, too.

Throughout the 1980s and 1990s, in-line skating continued to develop. People started catching on to the sport, and more companies began making in-line skates. Soon, hockey players, skiers, and racers adapted in-line skates for their own uses.

Today, in-line skating and roller-skating are very different. Not only has the equipment for both changed, but their styles and uses have changed as well. Skates have become lighter, faster, and cheaper. Today, millions of people around the world are in-line skating.

The Skate

Most in-line skates have boots, liners, brakes, wheels, and buckles or laces. The boot is the part of the skate that supports the foot and ankle. It is usually made of plastic, but it can also be made of leather or fabric.

Most boots are made up of a shell and a cuff. The shell covers the main part of the foot. The cuff wraps around the ankle. Most of today's recreational skates have hinged cuffs. The hinge allows a skater more **flexibility**, while still supporting the ankle and foot.

Inside, many in-line skates have a liner with a footbed attached. The liner looks like a large, stiff sock with a tongue. It can be padded with foam for comfort. The liner is removable and is an important part of how well the skate fits.

The bottom of the boot contains the skate's frame. It holds the wheels and brake. The brake is usually a rubber pad attached to the frame's heel. It can be attached to the right or left skate. The brake should be worn on the skater's dominant side.

Parts of an In-Line Skate

liner

cuff

hinge

boot

shell

buckle

heel brake

wheel

frame

Most recreational skates have four wheels. But skates for small feet may have only three wheels. Wheels come in different sizes. Small wheels are stable and allow a skater to turn easily. They are most often used by aggressive skaters who do tricks. Large wheels roll faster and are used by racers. Each wheel has small metal **bearings** inside of it. The bearings allow the wheels to roll smoothly. Bearings are rated by how well they roll. Bearings with higher numbers roll better. However, they are not necessarily better quality than bearings with lower ratings.

Buckles are supportive. They are often used on recreational skates.

Buckles or laces fasten the skate to the skater's foot. Buckles are adjustable. They are often the main support for the cuff. Laces are used to adjust the skate to fit the skater's foot. The main part of the boot may have either buckles or laces.

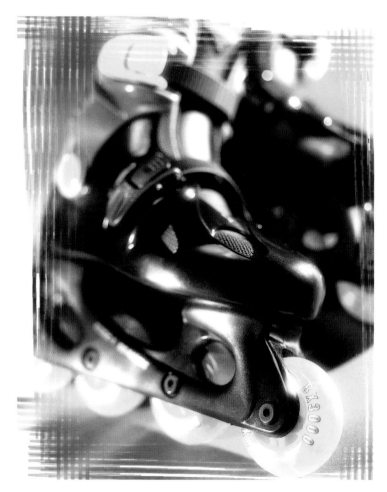

Buckles are easier to use than laces. That's because buckles don't change position. They also offer more support than laces. For these reasons, all beginner skates use buckles. Specialty skates often have laces. These skates are used by advanced skaters.

Gearing Up

Before you start in-line skating, you will need to find the proper gear. Fortunately, skates and safety equipment are all you need to get started. Before buying expensive gear, try renting it. Renting can help you decide if you like skating. It also allows you to try different styles and brands of skates.

When buying your own skates, first decide how you will use them. Some people use in-line skates for hockey, aggressive skating, or **cross-training**. Other people are recreational skaters. This style is a good way for beginners to start in-line skating.

Next, choose a high-quality skate. Cheap, low-quality skates usually don't fit well and may cause blisters. The frame should be sturdy, and the wheels should turn easily. However, the fit is the most important factor in choosing a good in-line skate.

14

When choosing skates, try on different brands and find the pair that fits your feet best. Be sure to wear the socks you will use while skating. Socks affect how well the skate fits. Wearing medium-weight athletic socks with thin liner socks underneath them is best.

Protective gear should be worn whenever you skate. This gear includes a helmet, elbow pads, knee pads, and wrist guards.

After the skates are fastened, they should feel snug but not uncomfortable. Skates should support your feet and ankles with no pressure or pain in either area. To check the fit, stand up, bend your knees, and move around.

Your feet shouldn't slide inside the boots. Your toes should lightly touch the end of the boots while standing. But when you bend your knees, your toes should move back slightly.

Safety equipment is the only other gear needed for in-line skating. Falling is a regular part of in-line skating, especially when you are first learning. So be sure to buy proper safety equipment. It should fit snugly, without feeling tight.

Safety equipment includes a helmet, knee pads, elbow pads, and wrist guards. The helmet is the most important piece of

safety gear. It should fit properly and be **certified** by a safety organization. Knee and elbow pads are usually padded with a hard outer cup. Wrist guards have hard plastic on the palm and wrist. This hard plastic protects a skater from injury.

In addition, reflective clothing or a light attached to your skate or helmet will help others see you when it is dark. Skating with the proper gear and common sense will help protect you from most injuries.

Rules of the Road

The best way to learn in-line skating is to take a lesson. A trained instructor will teach you how to start, stop, turn, and even fall! Learning basic moves will keep you and those around you safe.

Good places to skate include skateparks, bike paths, and empty parking lots. Skaters should also follow the International Inline Skating Association's rules of the road. Following these rules makes skating easier and safer. It also shows respect for other people.

First, skate intelligently. You can do this by always wearing protective gear. It is also important to keep all of your gear in good condition.

Second, skate legally. This is done by obeying community traffic laws. An in-line skater should follow the same laws as a bicyclist or **vehicle** driver.

Third, skate alertly. This means skating under control. Avoid skating in water, sand, and other debris. It's also important to stay away from busy roads or paths.

Finally, skate politely. Skate on the right side of the path and pass people on the left. Saying, "passing on your left," will inform people of your **intentions**. Lastly, always remember to yield to **pedestrians**.

Maintenance

In-line skates need regular care to keep them in good working condition. After each skating **session**, remove the liners to allow them to air out. Keep the boots, wheels, **bearings**, and frames clean by wiping them with a soft, damp cloth.

The brake and wheels will wear down with regular use. Replace the brake just before it reaches the halfway mark. To check the wheels, look down the frame from one end. If one side looks more worn than the other, the wheels need **rotating**.

The best way to maintain bearings is to stay away from sand, dirt, oil, or water when skating. To check the bearings, spin the wheels. They should spin easily and not make grinding noises. If necessary, it is possible to remove and clean or replace the wheels and bearings.

Stores that sell in-line skates will often do basic maintenance. This may include wheel rotation and bearing cleaning or replacement. Ask an adult or an employee at a skate shop for help or tips on maintenance.

Lingo

half-pipe

A half-pipe is a U-shaped ramp on which skaters do tricks.

fakie

A fakie is doing a trick while moving backward.

grind

This trick is done by sliding along a rail or other edge. Skaters who grind usually have a grind plate attached between their skates' wheels to protect the frames.

freestyle

This type of in-line skating is similar to ice-skating. It is also called artistic skating.

durometer

This rating describes the hardness of a wheel. The higher the number, the harder the wheel.

aggressive

In this skating style, skaters do tricks and stunts, usually on ramps or street courses.

heel stop

In a heel stop, the braking foot slides forward until the heel is even with the other skate's front wheel. The toe of the braking foot then lifts up, applying the brake.

ABEC

The Annular Bearing Engineering Council developed this rating scale for bearings. Ball bearings are rated ABEC-1, 3, 5, and 7. A rating of 7 rolls more easily than a 1.

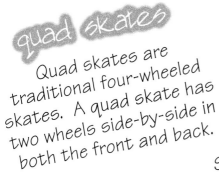

quad skates

Quad skates are traditional four-wheeled skates. A quad skate has two wheels side-by-side in both the front and back.

stair riding

This stunt is done when the skater rides down a set of stairs.

recreational

Skating for fun, without using specialized equipment or moves, is called recreational skating.

skatepark

A skatepark is an area specifically set up for skaters to practice in. It can be either indoors or outdoors.

road rash

The scrapes and burns a skater receives from falling on pavement without protective gear are called road rash.

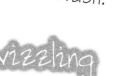

vert

The term vert is short for the word vertical. It can mean skating on ramps, pipes, or flat surfaces that angle up.

swizzling

To swizzle, a skater brings his or her feet together and then apart in order to move forward. This is done without lifting either skate off the ground. Swizzling produces an hourglass pattern on the ground.

T-stop

The T-stop allows a skate to stop without a brake. The skater slowly brings one foot behind the other foot to form a **T**. The wheels drag along the ground, which stops the skater.

23

Fabiola da Silva

Today, the world's best female aggressive skater is Fabiola da Silva. She was born in São Paulo, Brazil, in 1979. She began roller-skating at age eight. Two years later, her mother gave her a pair of in-line skates.

Soon, da Silva began to get noticed for her skills at aggressive skating. In 1996, da Silva was invited to participate in the X Games, where she won the gold medal. She soon became the only female on Team Rollerblade.

Da Silva continued to win female competitions. She has won the X Games five times. She's also won the Aggressive Skaters Association (ASA) World Championships three times.

Fabiola da Silva in competition

In 2000, the ASA eliminated the women's vert event. But they introduced a rule often called the Fabiola Rule. It allows women to enter the men's vert finals. Da Silva has placed in the top 10 of several men's vert events since then.

Fabiola da Silva is one of today's most respected skaters. "I believe that girls can do it," da Silva said, "and I am going to keep skating and trying my hardest. In the beginning it will be hard but in the future it's going to be good."

Fabiola da Silva

In-Line Skating Today

Many in-line skaters begin as recreational skaters and move on to other types of skating. Today, aggressive skating, speed skating, and in-line hockey are popular in-line sports. Each has developed its own distinct style.

Aggressive skating involves **stunts** such as jumping off ramps and riding rails. Skaters of this style can participate in events such as the X Games, the ASA Pro Tour, and the Gravity Games. Skaters Shane Yost, Marc Englehart, Takeshi Yasutoko, and Martina Svobodova are some of today's top aggressive skaters.

In-line speed skating has also become a separate sport. Speed skaters race on tracks or stretches of road. Speed skates have long frames that hold five wheels. The wheels are usually large, making the skates fast. In-line speed skaters from around the world compete in international competitions.

In-line hockey is popular with many skaters. This style developed from ice hockey as a way to train during the summer. Today, it is its own sport with rules based on its ice-hockey roots.

Today, millions of people are in-line skating. It is a sport that is growing in popularity worldwide. Not only is in-line skating a fun sport, but it is also good exercise. So choose your style and start skating!

Glossary

bearing - a machine piece that supports a moving part, allowing it to move more smoothly.

certify - to guarantee the quality of something.

cross-training - preparing for a sport by performing another activity or sport. For example, ice-hockey players cross-train by in-line skating.

flexible - able to bend without breaking.

intention - a planned act.

market - to sell or advertise a product.

pedestrian - a person who travels by walking.

rotate - to change in a fixed order.

session - a period of time spent performing an activity.

stunt - an act that is done to attract attention, especially one showing strength, skill, or courage.

vehicle - a car, truck, or bus.

Web Sites

Would you like to learn more
about in-line skating? Please
visit **www.abdopub.com** to find
up-to-date Web site links about
this sport and its competitions.
These links are routinely monitored and
updated to provide the most current
information available.

Index

A

Aggressive Skaters Association 26, 27, 28

B

bearings 8, 12, 20
Belgium 6
boots 8, 10, 13, 16, 20
brakes 7, 8, 10, 20
buckles 10, 13

C

Chicago Roller Skate Company 7, 8
competitions 4, 26, 27, 28

D

da Silva, Fabiola 26, 27

E

Englehart, Marc 28

F

Fabiola Rule 27
frame 10, 14, 20, 28
France 4, 6

I

ice hockey 8, 28
International Inline Skating Association 18

L

laces 10, 13
liners 10, 20
London, England 6

M

maintenance 20
Merlin, Joseph 6
Minnesota 8

N

Naegele, Bob Jr. 8

O

Olson, Brennan 8
Olson, Scott 8

P

Petitbled 6

R

Rollerblade 8
roller-skating 6, 7, 9, 26

S

safety gear 14, 16, 17, 18
São Paulo, Brazil 26
skateparks 18
skating styles 4, 8, 9, 12, 14, 26, 28, 29
Svobodova, Martina 28

T

Team Rollerblade 26

W

wheels 6, 7, 8, 10, 12, 14, 20, 28

Y

Yasutoko, Takeshi 28
Yost, Shane 28